THE SCROOBIOUS PIP

Edward Lear's

THE
SCROOBIOUS PIP

Completed by Ogden Nash

ILLUSTRATED BY NANCY EKHOLM BURKERT

HARPER & ROW, PUBLISHERS · NEW YORK, EVANSTON, AND LONDON

THE SCROOBIOUS PIP

FOR MY FAMILY AND FRIENDS

"—The sun is down! there is peace in nature, peace in my heart!—
The evening is so light!—We sail! The night is clear!—We sail!"

Hans Christian Andersen
A Poet's Bazaar

*F*OREWORD: *The Scroobious Pip*, like the stories of the Creation and Noah's Ark, stirs visions of all the creatures in the world assembled. Cast among them, however, is the unique and mysterious Pip.

The creator of the mysterious Pip was the English artist Edward Lear (1812-1888), famous for his nonsense books and increasingly well-known for his other accomplishments: his exceptionally fine illustrations of natural history, the oils and thousands of watercolors he painted as a "topographical landscape painter," and the seven travel books he wrote and illustrated.

He traveled constantly, spending many hours out of doors recording—in his drawings of the landscape or in his extensive journals—the infinite variety of nature. No subtlety of leaf, light, rock, or human existence escaped his perceptive brush and pen.

Edward Lear was the loyal friend of several leaders and creative artists of his day (among them Alfred, Lord Tennyson, whose work influenced Lear throughout his life), a welcome guest in their homes, and "Adopty Duncle" to their children. It was for these children that he composed his nonsense drawings and verses. How delightful it must have been to watch him as he drew or to listen as he invented hilarious new words—such as "pumptiliously" or "gromboolian"—and made fun of the world.

A lonely bachelor—often melancholy, too often separated from those he loved, subject to recurring illnesses—he spent some of the happiest hours of his life with the children he adored, secure in the merriment he created. But in these light-hearted hours he also released some of his darker thoughts, disguising them in humor. We can see Edward Lear himself in many of his nonsense drawings and in his longer poems such as *The Yonghy-Bonghy Bo*, *The Dong with the Luminous Nose*, *My Aged Uncle Arley*, and *Calico Pie*. We discover him again, but in a spirit of peace and optimism, in *The Scroobious Pip*.

One hundred years ago, in 1868, Edward Lear spent two months on the island of Corsica, where he made over three hundred drawings, continued his usual vast correspondence, and maintained his detailed journals. The manuscript for *The*

Scroobious Pip (with his own small pen drawing of the Pip on which I based my concept) is now to be found in Harvard University's Houghton Library in Cambridge, Massachusetts. The poem is written on the reverse of a page of notes from his Corsican tour and dated April 16, 17, 18. The verses were not completed, and they remained unpublished during his lifetime.

I am grateful that Ogden Nash—declaring himself "enormously pleased and flattered to be invited to fill in the empty squares of Mr. Lear's entrancing puzzle" —agreed to complete *The Scroobious Pip*, adding his own skillful fun to that of his "master's." Mr. Nash's additions are bracketed in the text.

During my research for this book I was astounded once again by the incredible number and variety of forms in nature. Of the multitude, I have been able to represent relatively few. We shall have to use our imaginations to complete the vision. For instance, nature offers us not only *one* species of zebra—there are several distinct kinds of zebra to treasure! And what sadness when one thinks of the extinct animals, when one learns that even in the one hundred years since *The Scroobious Pip* was written at least one hundred species of animals have become extinct. Many more are in danger now. In the future we shall still find certain kinds of whales in our oceans, but the largest creature that ever lived, that gentle mammal the Blue Whale, may soon be gone forever.

It would be in the spirit of Edward Lear to acknowledge and respect all the unique forms of nature. We *alone* are able to assume responsibility for preserving them.

It is this ideal of harmony between ourselves and nature which I feel is present in the rhythmic verses of *The Scroobious Pip* and which made me so want to illustrate them.

Nancy Burkert

London, April, 1968

THE SCROOBIOUS PIP

1

The Scroobious Pip went out one day
When the grass was green and the sky was gray.
Then all the beasts in the world came round
When the Scroobious Pip sat down on the ground.
      The cat and the dog and the kangaroo,
      The sheep and the cow and the guinea pig too,
      The wolf he howled, the horse he neighed,
      The little pig squeaked, and the donkey brayed,
      And when the lion began to roar
      There never was heard such a noise before.
      And every beast he stood on the tip
      Of his toes to look at the Scroobious Pip.

At last they said to the fox, "By far
You're the wisest beast. You know you are!
Go close to the Scroobious Pip and say,
Tell us all about yourself we pray—
For as yet we can't make out in the least
If you're fish or insect, or bird or beast."
The Scroobious Pip looked vaguely round
And sang these words with a rumbling sound,
   "Chippetty flip! Flippetty chip!
My only name is the Scroobious Pip!"

2

The Scroobious Pip from the top of a tree
Saw the distant Jellybolee—
And all the birds in the world came there,
Flying in crowds all through the air.
The vulture and eagle, the cock and the hen,
The ostrich, the turkey, the snipe, and the wren,
The parrot chattered, the blackbird sung,
And the owl looked wise but held his tongue,
And when the peacock began to scream
The hullabaloo was quite extreme.
And every bird he fluttered the tip
Of his wing as he stared at the Scroobious Pip.

At last they said to the owl, "By far
You're the wisest bird. You know you are!
Fly close to the Scroobious Pip and say,
Explain all about yourself we pray—
For as yet we have neither seen nor heard
If you're fish or insect, beast or bird!"
The Scroobious Pip looked gaily round
And sang these words with a chirpy sound,
　　　"Flippetty chip! Chippetty flip!
My only name is the Scroobious Pip!"

3

The Scroobious Pip went into the sea
By the beautiful shore of the Jellybolee—
All the fish in the world swam round
With a splashing, squashy, spluttering sound.
      The sprat, the herring, the turbot too,
      The shark, the sole, and the mackerel blue,
      The flounder sputtered, the porpoise puffed,
      [The tarpon tacked and the sailfish luffed,]
      And when the whale began to spout
      [They all gave a blubbly, glubbly shout.]
      And every fish he shook the tip
      Of his tail as he gazed on the Scroobious Pip.

At last they said to the whale, "By far
You're the biggest fish. You know you are!
Swim close to the Scroobious Pip and say,
Tell us all about yourself we pray—
For to know you yourself is our only wish;
Are you beast or insect, bird or fish?"
The Scroobious Pip looked softly round
And sung these words with a liquid sound,
    "Pliffity flip! Pliffity flip!
My only name is the Scroobious Pip!"

4

The Scroobious Pip sat under a tree
By the silent shores of the Jellybolee—
All the insects in all the world
About the Scroobious Pip entwirled.

> *Beetles and [bookworms] with purple eyes,*
> *Gnats and buzztilential flies,*
> *Grasshoppers, butterflies, spiders too,*
> *Wasps and bees and dragonflies blue,*
> *And when the gnats began to hum*
> *[The welkin] bounced like a dismal drum.*
> *And every insect curled the tip*
> *Of his snout and looked at the Scroobious Pip.*

At last they said to the ant, "By far
You're the wisest insect. You know you are!
Creep close to the Scroobious Pip and say,
Tell us all about yourself we pray—
For we can't find out, and we can't tell why—
If you're beast or fish, or a bird or a fly."
The Scroobious Pip turned quickly round
And sang these words with a whistly sound,
        "Wizzeby wip! Wizzeby wip!
My only name is the Scroobious Pip!"

5

Then all the beasts that walk on the ground
Danced in a circle round and round,
And all the birds that fly in the air
Flew round and round in a circle there,
And all the fish in the Jellybolee
Swum in a circle about the sea,
And all the insects that creep or go
Buzzed in a circle to and fro.
And they roared and sang and whistled and cried
Till the noise was heard from side to side,
"Chippetty tip! Chippetty tip!
Its only name is the Scroobious Pip!"

''CHIPPETTY TIP! CHIPPETTY TIP!

ITS ONLY NAME IS THE SCROOBIOUS PIP!''

Designed by Gloria Bressler and Nancy Ekholm Burkert
Set in Palatino Italic
Composed by The Composing Room, Inc.
Color separation and lithography by Neff Lithographing Company, Inc.
Bound by A. Horowitz & Son
The drawings were executed in brush and inks.
Harper & Row, Publishers, Incorporated